AMAZING STORIES® ☺ JUNIOR EDITION

Hudson's Bay Company Adventures

Tales of Canada's Early Fur Traders

by Elle Andra-Warner

Ab

To Canada's pioneers and Native peoples,
whose stories continue to inspire us
with their spirit of adventure.

PUBLISHED BY ALTITUDE PUBLISHING CANADA LTD.
1500 Railway Avenue, Canmore, Alberta T1W 1P6
www.altitudepublishing.com
www.amazingstories.ca
1-800-957-6888

Based on a book with the same title
by Elle Andra-Warner, first published in 2005.

Extreme care has been taken to ensure that all information presented in
this book is accurate and up to date. Neither the author nor the
publisher can be held responsible for any errors.

Publisher	Stephen Hutchings
Associate Publisher	Kara Turner
Junior Edition Series Editor	Linda Aspen-Baxter
Cover and Layout	Bryan Pezzi

We acknowledge the financial support of the Government
of Canada through the Book Publishing Industry Development
Program (BPIDP) for our publishing activities.

Altitude GreenTree Program
Altitude Publishing will plant twice as many trees as were used
in the manufacturing of this product.

ISBN 10: 1-55439-700-6
ISBN 13: 978-1-55439-700-6

Amazing Stories® is a registered trademark of Altitude Publishing Canada Ltd.

Printed and bound in Canada by Friesens
2 4 6 8 9 7 5 3 1

Note: Words in **bold** are defined in the glossary at the back of the book

Contents

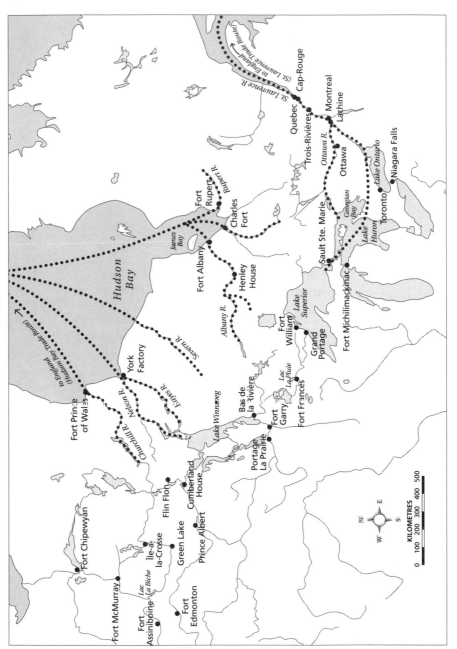

Hudson's Bay Company trade routes

Prologue

It was a tragic day at Seven Oaks, Manitoba. It was June 19, 1816. The Métis leader, Cuthbert Grant, and his men were armed for war. Many were painted with war paint. Grant was the captain general. He was leading over 60 Métis on horseback. They were going to capture Fort Douglas. It belonged to the Hudson's Bay Company. Fort Douglas was the centre of Selkirk's Red River settlement.

*The attack would not be a surprise. Governor Semple had already been warned about an attack. He had chosen to ignore the warning. Semple had a plan that he believed would work. His plan was to meet the attackers. He would read them the **proclamation** forbidding Métis to commit acts of violence against the **colony** ...*

* * *

Grant and his mounted riders arrive. He calls for the Métis to halt at the group of trees known as Seven Oaks. They position themselves in a half-moon formation. At the same time, Semple leads about 30 volunteers, on foot, out of the fort. In single file, they walk across the field to meet the Métis.

The Métis begin to tighten their half-circle. They

steer Semple and his men towards the river bank. Grant signals a Métis named Francois Boucher. Boucher is to order Governor Semple and his men to lay down their arms — or be shot. Boucher slowly brings his horse forward. Semple strides forward to meet him. He boldly seizes the bridle of Boucher's horse. Grant has his gun trained on Semple.

A heated discussion develops.

"What do you want?" asks Boucher in broken English.

"What do you want?" says Semple.

"We want our fort," replies Boucher.

"Well, go to your fort!" Semple yells back.

There is a scuffle as Semple tries to seize Boucher's gun. A shot rings out. Grant still has his gun on the governor. He pulls the trigger and wounds Semple in the thigh.

The fierce competition for the fur trade becomes warfare.

Chapter 1
From the Beaver to the HBC

The story of the North American fur trade began more than 500 years ago. It started because men wanted hats made of beaver.

There had been beavers in Europe and Russia. In the sixteenth century, they were trapped until they were almost **extinct**. Beaver skins, or pelts, were in high demand to make hats in England. Then European hatters discovered the superb fur of North American beavers. They wanted to get that fur to make their felt for hats. The richest, thickest beaver pelts came from the far north regions of North America. And the hatters wanted them.

The Native peoples welcomed fur trade with Europeans. They traded their beaver coats and pelts for goods, such as kettles, knives, and guns. These goods made their lives easier.

There was money to be made in the beaver trade. The English and the French became rivals in this trade. It also led to the formation of the Hudson's Bay Company (HBC).

The Hat That Started It All
People began to wear hats in Europe in the 1300s. It took another 100 years for hats to become popular. Men first made hats fashionable. The first men's beaver hats were made using the actual beaver skins. The "felted" hats appeared in Europe around 1456. They made their way to England about 50 years later. When the fine fur of the Canadian beaver became known in the 1600s, everyone wanted hats. Men's hats were more than fashion. They showed the social position of the men who wore them. The bigger the hat, the more important the wearer was.

The best hats were made from the fur of beaver pelts. They were strong and waterproof. They also had a rich shine. The European hatters made another discovery. The very best beaver pelts came from the "coat beaver." This was worn by Native peoples in North America. The Native peoples sewed six to eight pelts together to make their coat beaver. They used **sinew** for thread. The fur side of the pelts was worn next to their body. The sweat of their bodies mixed with the smoke of their lodges. This made the inside fur soft and silky. The pelt's long "guard hairs" fell out. Only the soft "underfur" was left. This downy fur soon became prized for making the beaver hats.

The first **cocked hats** were the Cavalier Hats of the 1600s. Gallant knights in England wore them. So did musketeers in France. These beaver hats had wide brims. They were trimmed with ostrich plumes and jewellery. One side of the brim was usually cocked or rolled. There was one problem. The droopy brims got in the way for horse riding and sword fighting.

Men's hats became more of a symbol of status. The cocked beaver hats grew bigger and higher. The 1700s brought the Tricorne Hats. These hats became popular in the American and French Revolutions. Gentlemen and nobles throughout Europe wore them. They were also worn by pirates. Around 1790, artists and scholars chose to wear the Bicorne Hat. It was also the military dress hat of the British, the American, and the French. Napoleon Bonaparte wore the Bicorne Hat. It was his signature hat.

For over 200 years, making hats with beaver felt was a growing industry. Good hatters made roughly nine hats a week. Five different groups of workers carried out 36 different steps to make one beaver hat. Women prepared the fibers and did the finishing work. Men bowed the fur into batts. They felted and fulled the batts into hats. Men also blocked, shaved, dyed, stiffened, and waterproofed them. The finest quality beaver hats had 255 to 340 grams of pure fur in them. It took four beaver pelts to produce 450 grams of the fine soft underfur.

The world of hat making was full of secret formulas. There were many rival hat makers. Hat shops developed their own ways of making hats. These became trade secrets. If an employee told these trade secrets to a competitor's shop, the punishment could be death.

There was always the danger of the mad hatter syndrome. Mercury caused heavy metal poisoning. The pelts were soaked in a solution of mercury (mercuric oxide). This made the fur come off the pelts easier. The process was called carroting because it gave fibres an orange tint. There was mercury in the steam coming off the felt. It attacked the central nervous system of the men who were felting and fulling the hats. This is where the term "mad as a hatter" came from.

Before the fur trade, there were roughly six million beavers in Canada. During the peak of the fur trade, more than 200,000 pelts a year were sold to Europe. Most pelts were made into hats. The value of a beaver hat depended on the supply and demand of the beaver pelts. When beaver hats were most popular, a hat would cost a skilled worker six month's wages. Fathers passed their beaver hats down to their sons. In 1659, Nantucket Island was purchased for £30 and two beaver hats. The hats were for the governor and his wife.

The cocked hat fell out of fashion in the 1800s. The tall Stovepipe Hat with its small rolled brim replaced it. Over time, the beaver pelt supply ran out in North America. Silk plush replaced beaver fur. The era of beaver hats drew to a close.

Beaver hats were the fashion rage in Europe for many years. Few Europeans had ever seen a live beaver. Few knew anything about the animal or its building skills.

The Incredible Canadian Beaver

The demand for beaver fur started the fur trade in North America. The beaver had an important place in Canadian history.

The beaver is the second largest rodent in the world. The adult weighs from 16 to 32 kilograms. It measures 1.3 metres long. Its legs are short so it moves slowly on land. In water, the beaver is a swift and graceful swimmer. Its 30-centimetre tail works as a four-way rudder. It can swim up to seven kilometres per hour. It has huge chisel-like teeth. These bright orange teeth are always growing. If the teeth are not worn down by gnawing, they will keep growing. In time, they will pierce the beaver's skull. The beaver will die.

Beavers are known for their building. They are architects and builders. They also plan and manage their environment. They build snug lodges with entrances. The inside of their lodges has a feeding chamber and a dry nest den. Lodges also have a system for bringing in fresh air. They use padded-down twigs and wide blades of grass for bedding. They change their bedding regularly. A family of five or six beavers lives in a lodge.

After freezing weather begins, the beaver goes to work. It plasters the lodge with mud, except for the air intake near the top. This makes an outer shell like concrete. Only humans can break it. The beaver protects the lodge further. It builds a network of beaver dams to control the water. They use sticks, rocks, and mud from the river bed to build the dams. The dams create deep water ponds. The beaver stores his winter food in these ponds. It eats mostly birch, cottonwood, poplar, willow, and young bark.

The beaver uses its engineering skills in another way. It also builds a canal system. Ditches redirect water and collect it from swamps. The canals can be 1.5 metres wide, 1 metre deep, and more than 182 metres long. The beaver transports food supplies along the canals.

Beavers became pets at some of the HBC posts. Samuel Hearne was governor of Fort Prince of Wales from 1775 to 1782. He had several beavers in his tiny private zoo. He wrote about his beavers in his journal. They became so tame that they answered to their names. They even followed him around. "They were as pleased at being fondled as any animal I ever saw. During the winter they lived on the same food as the women. They were very fond of rice and plum pudding."

Edward Umfreville was a fur trader. He also wrote

about a beaver as a pet. "I once had a young male which, after a month's keeping, would follow me about like a dog. When I had been absent from him for a couple of hours, he would show as much joy at my return as a dog could possibly do."

The beaver became the official emblem of Canada. It was recognized as a symbol of the independence of Canada by Royal Assent in a 1975 Act.

Indigenous Trappers and Traders
Native peoples had been trapping the beaver for thousands of years. They used all the parts. The skins were used for clothing. The meat was used for food. Medicine was made from beaver castoreum, a strong-smelling substance. They traded the pelts to other native groups. Trade networks were set up all over the continent. The Native peoples had a successful trading system long before the Europeans began to trade. In the beginning, the Europeans were just another trading partner.

Each year, Native peoples gathered in places across North America. They would come together to trade and fish. They would also celebrate. Trading links were well known. So were the trading routes. They followed the natural waterways of lakes and rivers.

Kay-Nah-Chi-Wan-Nung was one of those gathering places. It was located on North America's oldest highway. It was called Gete Miikana. This is Ojibway for The Old Road. This travel route stretched from northern

Minnesota to the Manitoba border. For over 6000 years, Gete Miikana linked a trading network that spread across the continent. Thousands paddled each year to Kay-Nah-Chi-Wan-Nung. They camped along the shores of the Rainy River.

The Native peoples fished for lake sturgeon with spears and hooks. They planted summer gardens. Men played the traditional moccasin game. And they traded using a bartering system. Each native group traded different goods. The goods depended on where they lived on the continent. Obsidian from Wyoming. Copper from Lake Superior. Marine shells from Florida. Turquoise from the southwestern United States. Flint from the Dakotas. Fish oil from the Pacific. Furs from the north.

Some tribes became middlemen. They developed trading empires. A tribe of Plains Native peoples operated the Mandan trading empire. At one time, it covered a huge area of North America. It went north from present-day Saskatchewan and Alberta. It stretched east to Lake of the Woods and from the Missouri River to Mexico. As middlemen, they held trade fairs. These traders knew what they were doing. They would buy a horse from one trading partner. Then they would sell it to another partner for double its price.

Arrival of New Trade Partners
Then the Europeans arrived in northern Canada. They met native buyers who were careful and clever. The

Native peoples knew how to bargain with English and French traders. They refused items they didn't need. They refused items that were not good enough. They knew when the Europeans tried to trade guns that didn't work properly. They could tell when the Europeans tried to trade water-damaged tobacco.

The Native peoples helped the Europeans. They taught them how to survive in the wilderness. They showed them how to make birch-bark canoes and moccasins. They taught them how to make snowshoes and toboggans. They showed them the best natural waterway routes. They explained the habits of the animals the Europeans needed for food. They showed them how to make clothing from deer and caribou hides. They showed the Europeans how to harvest rice. They taught them to make pemmican. Dried meat, fat, and berries were used to make pemmican. It became the basic food of the inland fur trade.

From the beginning, the Europeans and the Native peoples had a trading relationship that worked. The traders needed to supply Europe with beaver. They needed the Native peoples to provide them with beaver.

Chapter 2
The Launch of a Trading Empire

The Hudson's Bay Company was a great trading empire. It began with two brave French fur traders. They were Pierre-Esprit Radisson and Médard Chouart, Sieur des Groseilliers.

Radisson and des Groseilliers had a dream. Northern Canada had lots of beaver and other furs. They wanted to set up a great fur trading system. Ships would sail from Europe into the Hudson Bay. There, they would collect furs from trading posts. Native peoples would provide these furs for trade. Radisson and des Groseilliers dreamed of making lots of money with the fur trade.

A Plan Takes Shape

They had to set their plan in motion. Radisson and des Groseilliers had to make their first voyage to Hudson Bay. If it was successful, people would invest money in their plan. Before that ... they needed money to pay for the first voyage.

Their dream began in the early 1650s. It started in the area now known as the Great Lakes. Des Groseilliers was a powerful fur trader in Trois-Rivières. He was also clever and tough. Native peoples had told him stories about rich beaver country north of Lake Superior. This area hadn't been trapped. The stories interested him. Over the years, he learned more from his native trading partners.

French fur traders competed for new trade routes. They all wanted to find new routes. More routes meant more beaver pelts. The French governed the colony. The government held all the power. They made the rules and regulations to license traders. Des Groseilliers didn't like that. He didn't like being told what to do by anyone.

By August 1659, des Groseilliers and Radisson wanted to reach the Great Lakes with their native trading partners. This trip would put them into a good position for their Hudson Bay project. They went to the governor of New France to make their request. Could they go with the Hurons into the interior? He refused. They asked a second time to go with six Saulteaux.

The governor said yes, but they had to do one thing. A Jesuit priest had to go with them. There was no way des Groseilliers was going to accept this.

A Sneaky Departure

Radisson and des Groseilliers did not want to take a Jesuit priest. They slipped away one summer night in 1659. Saulteaux guides were waiting for them along the St. Lawrence River.

The journey was dangerous. New France was at war with the Iroquois. There were many attacks. Des Groseilliers was experienced in fighting against the Iroquois. His native partners respected his courage. They even thought of him as a "warrior chief." He broke through Iroquois ambushes by direct assault. One time, he hid himself behind bales of fur.

By October 1659, they had reached the far southwest of Lake Superior. They spent the winter with the Saulteaux, Menominee, and Dakotas. They fought with their Saulteaux allies against the Iroquois. Radisson and des Groseilliers had a strong bond with the Native peoples. It was based on trust. They even took part in a traditional celebration. It was the Algonquin "Feast of the Dead." This feast was held in Saulteaux territory at the end of the winter. Over 2000 people from 18 different nations came to the ceremonies. They lasted 14 days.

During the feast, Radisson and des Groseilliers

saw the Grand Assembly of the Algonquin peoples. They watched as the Sioux and Cree tribes made peace. Radisson and des Groseilliers spoke to the nations at the feast. They talked about how the nations would gain from trading with them. The two Frenchmen began a small trading fort in the territory.

A year later, Radisson and des Groseilliers returned to Trois-Rivières. It was August 19, 1660. Behind them was a fleet of 60 canoes and over 300 Assiniboine. In the canoes were bales of the shiniest beaver pelts ever. They were ready to talk to the governor of New France. They were going to ask him for ships and money for their next **expedition**. It would be a voyage to the Hudson Bay. They thought they could reach the bay by way of the Atlantic Ocean.

Radisson wrote about their return. "We finally reached Quebec ... We were greeted by several cannon blasts from the fort's battery and from some ships anchored in the harbour. These ships would have returned to France empty if we had not shown up."

The governor's response shocked them. He took away most of their pelts. They had left the colony without his permission. For that, he also made them pay huge taxes on their furs.

Des Groseilliers was furious. He sailed to France. He took his case to a higher court. He won. He got back the money he had paid in taxes.

A Radical Change of Direction

It was the summer of 1661. Des Groseilliers sailed back to New France. He and Radisson made a big decision. They would take their fur trading proposal to the English for support.

First, they went to New England. They talked to merchants in Boston. They wanted the merchants to invest in their plan. They gave Radisson and des Groseilliers some money.

Radisson and des Groseilliers began a trip to the Hudson Bay. Zachary Gillam was their captain. However, they had to call off the trip. It wasn't the end of their plan. There was still hope. Sir George Cartaret heard about their voyage. He was a member of the Court of King Charles II of England. He invited Radisson and des Groseilliers to present their plan to the king. In 1665, they set sail for England.

Bad luck followed them as they sailed across the Atlantic Ocean. Their ship was captured by Dutch privateers. They were held prisoner. Later they were put ashore in Spain. They finally got to England in the fall of 1665.

Radisson and des Groseilliers sailed up the Thames River to London. They passed barges anchored in midstream. Smoke surrounded the barges. Families were crowded on the barges. They were trying to avoid the bubonic plague. The plague killed many, many people. Radisson and des Groseilliers were given perfumed handkerchiefs to put over their noses. This was to cut the smell of rotting bodies. Victims of the plague were dumped in pits. The smell of death was everywhere.

Radisson and des Groseilliers met one setback after another. There was a strong feeling against the French in England at that time. The French were accused of starting the London fire of 1666. England was at war with the Dutch from 1665 to 1668. During this time, the Dutch fleet sailed right up the Thames River. They destroyed the navy line of defence. They also captured the Royal Navy flagship.

Radisson and des Groseilliers didn't give up. They kept working to get support. They said the right things. They made contacts with important people. They even started rumours. The Hudson Bay Project would make its investors rich. It might even lead the way to a northwest passage.

All their talking paid off. Powerful people in London began to believe in their plan. Even King Charles II supported them. Radisson and des Groseilliers were ready. They would lead England to the territories north of New France.

The Historic *Nonsuch* Voyage

Two ships were made ready for the journey to the Hudson Bay. One was the *Nonsuch*. The other was the *Eaglet*. Captain Zachary Gillam commanded the *Nonsuch*. Des Groseilliers sailed with him. Captain William Stannard commanded the *Eaglet*. Radisson sailed with him.

The *Nonsuch* on its first voyage

The British had sailed to the Hudson Bay before. The bay was named for Henry Hudson. He had entered the bay in 1610 on the *Discovery*. This voyage ended in **mutiny**. Hudson's crew rose up against him in 1611. They forced Hudson, his young son, and several crew members into a small boat. They set them adrift on the ice-filled bay. They were never seen again.

Others had also sailed the Hudson Bay. All spoke of how remote and out-of-the-way it was. No one had sailed to the bay for 25 years. It was a dangerous place. If there was wind, a captain had some control. If there was no wind, ships would drift. Then they would risk hitting huge ice floes.

These dangers did not stop Radisson and des Groseilliers. In June 1668, the *Nonsuch* and the *Eaglet* sailed from England. They reached the open sea and headed north. They went around the Orkneys and headed west toward the New World. (The Orkneys are a group of Islands at the far northern tip of Scotland.) Radisson and des Groseilliers were confident. Their mission would be a success.

It did not take long for trouble to strike. There was a terrible storm off Ireland. The *Eaglet* needed repairs. Radisson had to return to Plymouth with this ship. Des Groseilliers kept going with the *Nonsuch*, He reached James Bay in September 1668. It was three months after they had left England. The crew carried supplies ashore at the mouth of a river. They named this site Rupert's River. They had a wide range of supplies. They carried ashore tar, compasses, medicines, axes, saws, hammers, **blunderbusses**, muskets, pistols, powder, shot, beef, peas, oatmeal, raisins, prunes, sugar, spice, oil, lemon juice, paper, quills, eel nets, beer, and brandy.

A Successful Return

Radisson and des Groseilliers cleared the land of spruce trees. Then they built a house of upright logs. They filled the spaces between the logs with moss. A roof was made from local hatch. They named the house Charles Fort in honour of the king.

The crew had to survive the long winter. They fished the river for pike. They killed hundreds of geese and ptarmigans. They also built a cellar to store their beer. The men spent the winter of 1668–1669 at Charles Fort. In the spring, almost 300 Cree from James Bay came to trade.

The crew headed home on June 14, 1669. They were loaded with a cargo of fine beaver pelts. The cargo sold for over £1375. When all expenses were added up, the voyage had not made a profit. Despite this, the *Nonsuch* had returned safely with the highest quality furs. This proved the Hudson Bay Project was possible. Prince Rupert led the group that provided money for the voyage. (Prince Rupert was the cousin to King Charles II.) These investors were pleased. They were ready to outfit further expeditions.

Chapter 3
The Early Days of the HBC

O n May 2, 1670, King Charles II granted a Royal Charter to the new company. It was officially known as The Governor and Adventurers Trading in the Hudson Bay. Later, it would be known as the Hudson's Bay Company. The charter was written on five sheepskin papers. It had over 7000 words of handwritten text. The charter stated the new company's three goals. The first goal was fur-trading. The second was exploring for minerals. The third goal was to find a northwest passage.

Prince Rupert was one of the owners. There were 17 others. In June, the first woman **shareholder** signed on. She was Lady Margaret Drax. That made a total of 19 shareholders.

The king gave the new company a gift. He gave it

sole ownership of all the seas, waters, lakes, and lands of the Hudson Bay and its drainage system. It was one of the most generous gifts ever given by a king.

King Charles gave the new company a huge area of land. It covered 3.8 million square kilometres. The land stretched from Labrador to the Canadian Rockies. It included present-day Quebec and Ontario, all of Manitoba, southern Saskatchewan, and Alberta. It also took in the eastern part of the Northwest Territories. Much of Minnesota and North Dakota was also part of this area. The area was equal to almost 40 percent of modern-day Canada.

It was a vast new territory. The company had power to establish and enforce laws. It could build forts. It could have its own soldiers and maintain a navy. It could also make peace — or war — with the Native peoples. The company could run its empire any way it wanted. This land was to be called Rupert's Land. It was named after Prince Rupert. He had been the chief supporter of the company.

The Adventurers Spring Into Action
Radisson and des Groseilliers spent the winter in London in 1670–1671. When spring came, they were restless. These were men of action. Time was moving on. A month after the company received its Charter, they sailed back to the bay. They sailed with two ships. One was the *Prince Rupert*. It was commanded

by their old friend, Captain Gillam. The ship carried des Groseilliers and Thomas Gorst. The *Wivenhoe* was commanded by Captain Newlands. It sailed with Radisson and Charles Bayly. He was the first overseas governor of the new company.

Again, tragedy struck. Newlands got the *Wivenhoe* through the dangerous waters of the Hudson Straits. Then he died of scurvy. The crew buried him at Charles Fort in October 1670. Captain Newlands was the first European to be buried there. It was a sad beginning to the expedition.

They landed on the mouth of the Nelson River. Bayly nailed the King's Arm to a tree. This claimed the territory for England. The crew had to build a fort on the Nelson River. Bayly was to govern the region for the HBC from that fort. But it didn't happen.

A strong wind drove the *Wivenhoe* back into deep water. This forced the crew to sail eastward across the bay to join the other ship. It was a distance of 1158 kilometres. Both crews spent the winter at Charles Fort. It was at the lower end of the bay. Charles Fort was later called Rupert's House.

There was a lot of work to do during the long dark winter. A shallop was built to sail goods and people in the area. This small, light boat used a sail or oars. It was called the *Royal Charles*. In January, Radisson left to explore Moose River. He was to be gone three months. While he was gone, the governor kept the local Native peoples busy. He kept them hunting fresh meat to ward off scurvy.

From Madman to Governor

Charles Bayly was a strange choice for governor. He had just come from jail. He had played with King Charles II as a child. Some say this was why he was chosen. His mother was French. She was a lady-in-waiting to Charles' mother, Henrietta Maria. She was daughter of Henry IV of France.

Bayly's early years were filled with adventure. He was still a teenager when he was shipped overseas to Virginia. (Virginia was an English-American colony then.) He was a bond servant there for 14 years. While there, it is said he met Elizabeth Harris. She was a Quaker missionary. The Quakers were a religious group in America. They protested against church rules and customs. They believed each human being could contact God directly. Bayly became a Quaker.

In time, Bayly returned to Europe. He went to Rome. There, he met up with John Perrot. He was another Quaker believer. They wanted the pope to become a Quaker. Both men were put in a madhouse. Bayly protested. He refused to eat for 20 days. Bayly and Perrot were thrown out of Italy. To rebel, Bayly walked barefoot across France. He was often arrested and jailed. Finally, he returned to England. He ended up in dungeons and prisons there as well. While he was in prison, he wrote letters to King Charles II. Sometimes his letters warned the king to change his ways. King Charles kept him in the Tower of London from 1663 to 1669. Most thought he was insane. Bayly became known as "an old Quaker with a long beard."

Then a strange thing happened. In 1669, the king let Bayly go free. There was one condition. He had to go to Hudson Bay. He became the first overseas governor of the Hudson's Bay Company. For the next nine years, he did a good job of doing business. Bayly set up posts at the mouths of the major rivers flowing into the James and Hudson Bays. He started a supply depot on Charlton Island in James Bay. He planned the HBC's factory system. He traded fairly with the Native peoples.

The HBC'S First Auction

In 1671, the HBC ships left the bay. They were filled with a rich harvest of fur. They arrived back in London in October. The company decided to sell the pelts in two fur auctions at Garraway's Coffee House. It was near the Royal Exchange in London. The first HBC sale was posted for January 24, 1672. Some of the country's most powerful people went to the coffee house. It was a good place to sell furs … and make lots of money.

The bidding was done by candle. This was done in two ways. A two-and-a-half-centimetre candle was lit. Bids were made. When the candle went out, the highest bidder got the goods. In the second way, a pin was stuck into the candle. When the candle melted down and the pin fell out, the highest bidder got the goods. The best of English society went to the bidding at Garraway's. Prince Rupert was there. So was his cousin, the Duke of York.

The HBC sent another expedition in 1672. It arrived at Fort Charles in September. There were problems between Bayly and Radisson and des Groseilliers. Bayly didn't like the two Frenchmen. That was no secret. He kept telling them that he was the governor. He closely watched what they were doing. This bothered them, and he knew it. He did it anyway. Radisson and des Groseilliers didn't trust Bayly at all. They distrusted him so much, they left the HBC they had helped found.

It was early winter of 1672–1673. The Native peoples around Fort Charles were more on their guard with the English. They had met with Frenchmen in the area. These Frenchmen had warned them not to trust the English. The Frenchmen had told them that English guns were bewitched. Their religion was evil. Bayly began to worry. Were the Native peoples going to attack Fort Charles? He began to make the fort stronger.

The winter passed. Nothing happened. In March, six native **ambassadors** came to the fort. They announced that their chief, Kas-Kidi-dah, would soon be there. The chief arrived the next day. He brought a group with him, but very few beaver. Governor Bayly and Radisson were not at the fort that day. They were out hunting together. It wasn't because they were friends. Bayly didn't trust

Radisson at the fort without him. When one left the fort, they went together.

Captain Cole was in charge that day. Cole panicked because there were so many Native peoples tenting around the fort. When it was dark, he sent two men to look for the governor. Chief Kas-Kidi-dah also sent two of his men to look for Bayly.

When the governor returned, Radisson was not with him. Bayly didn't explain. The next day there was a rumour going around the fort. Bayly and Radisson had argued in the wilderness. The argument led to blows. Finally Radisson had tried to shoot Bayly.

Des Groseilliers was alarmed. Was this the true story? Bayly wouldn't say if the rumour was true or not. Des Groseilliers met with Chief Kas-Kidi-dah in the chief's wigwam. There, he finally learned where his partner was. The chief told him about a French post on the banks of the Moose River. It was an eight-day journey from Rupert River. He said Radisson had headed there. He planned to make his way back to New France.

Des Groseilliers and Bayly stayed another winter. There was still conflict between them. Des Groseilliers began to suspect Bayly. Had he been trying to drive both him and Radisson out of the HBC all along?

It was early April 1674. There was talk of a raid on the fort by hostile Native peoples in the area. Bayly, des Groseilliers, and Cole held a meeting. How would they protect themselves against such an attack? The Native peoples would leave the region to hunt. When that happened, they would head for the Moose River. It wasn't until the end of May that the HBC men could head out. At the last moment, Bayly said he wasn't going. He stayed at Fort Charles.

The group arrived at the mouth of the Moose River. Soon after, a band of Tahiti Native peoples came to trade 200 beaver pelts. During the trading ceremony, the chief of the Tahitis stared at des Groseilliers. Then he suddenly stopped the trading. The Englishman asked why. The chief said he recognized des Groseilliers. He was a Frenchman the chief had traded with many years ago. Des Groseilliers agreed they had met before. He told the chief not to be alarmed. He was trading as an "Englishman" with the HBC. He wasn't working on his own as a fur trader. The chief was still hostile. He told des Groseilliers, "You drove hard bargains. You took our silkiest, softest, and richest furs. In return, you gave us but beads and ribbons."

Des Groseilliers was an experienced fur trader. He didn't worry about the charges. He knew how to work the situation. He told the chief again that he was trading as an Englishman with the HBC. Trading continued. However, the damage had been done.

They returned to the fort. Bayly was told the Tahitis had refused to deal with des Groseilliers. Bayly decided to check it out. He arrived at Moose River. At the same time, a nation from Albany arrived to trade with him. He traded over 1500 beaver pelts. Later, he travelled along the coast. He met other native groups. They told him they would take their furs to the HBC instead of to the French.

Bayly returned to Fort Charles in July. The situation at the fort was tense. Des Groseilliers and Gorst were fighting. The HBC staff was close to mutiny. They didn't want to serve under a Frenchman.

A few days later, a Jesuit priest arrived at the fort. His name was Father Albanel. He gave Bayly a letter from Governor Talon in Quebec. Bayly was thrilled with the letter. Talon said, "from one great man to another." Bayly read the letter out loud at the fort so everyone could hear. The letter asked Bayly to treat Father Albanel politely. Bayly did so.

Later that evening, Bayly learned that Father Albanel had also delivered letters to des Groseilliers. Bayly thought he had been betrayed. The visit by Father Albanel was a trick to capture the fort and let it be robbed by hostile Native people. He ordered des Groseilliers brought to him. Gorst told him that the Jesuit priest and des Groseilliers were walking and chatting. Bayly went out and found them himself. He confronted des Groseilliers. He yelled and screamed at him. Finally, des Groseilliers had had enough. He knocked the governor down. Des Groseilliers returned calmly to the fort. He took his things and wages. He set off on an overland journey to Quebec with four men.

By December 1675, both Radisson and des Groseilliers had cut their ties with the HBC.

Des Groseilliers stayed at Trois-Rivières in Quebec. Radisson sailed with the French Navy until he was shipwrecked in 1679. He then made his way to Paris and on to England.

Were Radisson and des Groseilliers finished with the HBC? More adventures were to come.

Chapter 4
Standoff

It was the winter of 1682–1683 on the Hudson Bay. It was one of the strangest in the history of fur trading. It began in August 1682. Two old French sailing boats arrived at the mouth of the Nelson and Hayes Rivers. Their sea journey had been difficult. They had come through rough water and dangerous ice. Two **mutinies** had been attempted. The vessels reached Hayes River. Then they sailed 24 kilometres upstream. There, they set up a fur trading post. The 50-tonne *St. Pierre* had a crew of 12. The *St. Anne* carried 15 men. Their commanders were Radisson and des Groseilliers! This time, they were representing Compagnie du Nord. It was a French fur trading company. They had just started it with partners from New France. They would be **rivals** with the HBC.

The crews set to work to build Fort Bourbon on the south side of Hayes River. Radisson and his son, Jean-Baptiste, went to explore farther upstream. They made contact with some native hunters. They returned on September 12. They were back for only a short time when they heard the sound of a distant cannon …

The New Englanders
Someone else was sailing in this remote area of the world. Who was it? Radisson canoed to the mouth of the river to check. He spotted a tent on a small island in the Nelson River. He saw a group of men building a log house.

In the morning, Radisson paddled towards the camp. He stayed some distance from the shore. Radisson hailed them. He spoke first in French. Then he spoke in English. He asked what they were doing there.

They called back, "We are English and come for the beaver trade. We are from New England."

Radisson told them they had no right to be there. He said that he had discovered the area a few years before. He had claimed the area for the French. He told them to leave.

As Radisson was talking, his canoe drifted close to shore. He recognized the leader of the group in camp. It was Benjamin Gillam. He was the youngest son of his old friend, Captain Zachary Gillam. They embraced warmly. However, Radisson was careful. Gillam invited

Radisson on his ship. Radisson accepted. First, he kept two of Gillam's crew on shore as hostages.

Radisson bluffed Gillam during their meeting. He claimed there were massive French forces on the river. He told Gillam they had "absolute power" over the Native peoples. He gave Gillam permission to stay the winter. (It was too late in the season to safely sail out.) Radisson told Gillam he could keep building the log fort. It could not be fortified. They parted on fairly friendly terms.

The French party returned to their canoe. They headed back to the fort. Gillam's presence was a problem, but Radisson had things under control.

Things were about to get more complicated on the two rivers.

The HBC Returns to the Nelson River

On September 7, Radisson was paddling northward. There was another surprise. He saw a HBC ship heading up the Nelson River. Quickly, the French crew went ashore. They started a huge bonfire. Thick columns of smoke rose in the air. The HBC crew saw the smoke. They dropped anchor for the night. They thought the smoke was from a native camp.

Captain Zachary Gillam was on the HBC ship, the *Prince Rupert*. He had been to the mouth of the Nelson River in 1670. Radisson and Charles Bayly had sailed with him that time. They had wanted to set up a main HBC post on the Nelson River. That try had failed. It was 12 years later. Gillam was back to complete the task. Another HBC man was with him. John Bridgar was the governor for the new fort. It would be called Port Nelson.

Gillam knew that he and his crew would be there for the winter. His son Benjamin and 14 New Englanders were with him. Benjamin had licenses from the governor of Massachusetts to trade furs in the area.

The HBC had sent five ships to the area that year. Two of these were the *Prince Rupert* and the *Albercome*. They were ordered to go to the Nelson and Hayes Rivers to establish Port Nelson. Only Gillam's ship arrived …

Old Friends Meet Again

The next morning, the HBC ship sent a boat to investigate. Radisson was armed and ready. He was about to try bluffing again. He strode out to the shore to greet the strangers.

As the boat neared, he yelled out in English, "Hold, in the king's name. I forbid you to land." He showed his gun.

HBC Governor Bridgar was the group's leader. He told Radisson they were Englishmen. He asked him who he was and what business he had in stopping them.

Radisson replied, "I am a Frenchman. I hold this country for this Most Christian Majesty, King Lewis!" Two other Frenchmen in his party made a show of force. They came out of the woods, waving their weapons.

Bridgar stood up in his boat. He announced, "I beg

to inform you, gentlemen, that we hail from London. Our ship yonder is the *Prince Rupert*. It belongs to the honourable Hudson's Bay Company. It is commanded by Captain Zachary Gillam."

"You arrive too late," yelled Radisson. "This country is already in the possession of the King of France."

Bridgar invited Radisson to talk more on board the *Prince Rupert*. Radisson accepted. As before, his men held two Englishmen on shore as hostages.

On board the ship, Radisson bragged to Bridgar and Gillam. He said that he had two ships close by. He was expecting a third French ship any day. He was also building a huge fort. Bridgar listened. He pretended to be impressed. After Radisson left, he ignored Radisson's threats. He sent his men on shore to build Port Nelson, on the north side of the Nelson River.

The fall brought severe weather. Autumn gales on the Hudson Bay were harsh. And on October 21, 1682, there was a terrible storm. High winds whipped up huge waves. The strong currents made the seas dangerous. During this storm, the *Prince Rupert*'s anchor came loose. The ship was blown out to sea and sank. Captain Zachary Gillam drowned. So did several crew members.

A Challenging Winter
Radisson and des Groseilliers knew they couldn't beat their rivals by bluffing. They had to do better than that.

They had more trade experience. They knew more about the bush. They would be better traders. That's exactly what they did. They kept the control, and they made money from furs. Des Groseilliers and his son carried out the fur trading. Radisson spied on the two groups of English. Radisson travelled between the three forts to keep an eye on the English. Sometimes he put himself in great danger.

Radisson kept control of the area by outwitting the HBC men. Once he thought they were defying his authority. He invited Benjamin Gillam for a month's visit at the French fort. Then he took him prisoner. Radisson and nine of his men went to Gillam's fort. There was no resistance. They seized Gillam's fort and his ship.

Finally, in the summer of 1683, Radisson took control of the HBC's Port Nelson. He learned that Governor Bridgar had planned a night attack on Fort Bourbon. This was Radisson's own fort. Radisson turned the tables on the governor. He marched to Port Nelson with 12 men. He seized Bridgar's fort. He took the governor back to Fort Bourbon as a prisoner.

Living on the Edge
Radisson and des Groseilliers had the forts and pelts. They had the HBC men and the New Englanders. Next, they had to sell their furs to European customers. They also needed to transport some of their prisoners to New France. (These prisoners were Bridgar, young Gillam,

and the New Englanders). The other prisoners were allowed to return to their HBC posts on James Bay. Once again, things did not go the way they were planned.

During spring breakup, the two French ships were destroyed. They built one ship out of the two wrecks. The ships left the Nelson River. On July 27, one ship became jammed in the ice of the Hudson Bay. The ship sailing alongside it was split open. They had to stay there, surrounded by ice floes until August 24.

Finally, in October, they reached their destination. The French tax collector was waiting for them. He charged a 25 percent tax on the furs. He also took control of the ship. Again, New France was messing with the profits of Radisson and des Groseilliers.

Radisson and des Groseilliers weren't quite finished with the HBC yet. Within a year, the HBC offered to rehire them both. Des Groseilliers said no. He returned to domestic life. Radisson accepted. He became the superintendent and director of trade.

The next year Radisson returned to the Hudson Bay. He brought back over 20,000 beaver pelts for the HBC. His last voyage in 1687 was short, and he kept a low profile. His life was at risk for being a traitor to France. French commandos were looking for him.

Chapter 5
The Commando Raids

When Radisson agreed to work for the HBC, he offended the people of New France. In 1685, the citizens burnt an image of Radisson and des Groseilliers. A decree was given out for their arrest.

People at La Compagnie du Nord were also angry. Radisson had helped start La Compagnie du Nord in 1682. He had started the company to challenge HBC. The people at La Compagnie du Nord wanted something done. They asked the governor of New France to take military action. Governor Jacque-Rene de Brisay gave them what they wanted.

The Expedition
De Brisay ordered a military expedition. It had two

goals. The first was to drive the English out of the northern bays. The second was to capture the HBC forts. The governor appointed Chevalier Pierre de Troyes as the unit's commander. De Troyes had come to New France only eight months before. He was the captain of the colony's marines. He was a good commander. He was brave. He was strict with his men. He was a good planner. He could also be creative if needed. Some said he was looking for a chance to become a hero. He wanted to make his mark in history.

The governor gave de Troyes a lot of power. He was to "search for, seize and occupy the best posts. He was to seize the robbers, bush rangers, and others ... We order him to arrest Radisson and his supporters wherever they may be found. He was to bring them to be punished as deserters." The penalty for deserters was death.

De Troyes put together a small but strong military unit of 107 men. There were 30 French soldiers, 70 Canadian irregulars, six native guides, and one Jesuit priest, Father Sylvie. Three brothers were de Troyes's lieutenants. They had grown up in the area of the fur trade. There were expert bush rangers. The eldest was 25-year-old Pierre Le Moyne d'Iberville. (He would later become one of Canada's most famous naval commanders.) The other two were Paul Le Moyne de Maricourt and Jacques Le Moyne de Sainte Helene.

The commando unit left Montreal on March 3, 1686. They tramped northward on snowshoes along the frozen Ottawa River. They dragged sleds and 35 canoes behind them. The trip was an epic overland journey of over 1200 kilometres. They travelled north to James Bay.

It was a difficult trek. No large expeditions had travelled this way to the northern bays. The men had to deal with the dangers of the spring break-up. They had to detour around ice. They had to cut **portage** pathways. They had to struggle overland and get through rapids. They had to repair damaged canoes. They stumbled over rotten logs, fallen trees, and slippery rocks. They struggled through dense underbrush. Near the end of the journey, they fought large hordes of black flies.

By June 19, it had been 82 days since they left Montreal. The commando unit was near Moose Factory. This was the first HBC fort. De Troyes wasted no time. He led a scouting mission and located the fort on a large island in the Moose River. He decided to attack the next day. The troop built a battering ram. They sharpened the blades of their swords.

All the while, the Cree watched the Frenchmen. The local HBC had not treated them well. They were angry. As the French troops prepared for assault, the Cree stayed silent. The attackers crept close and quietly surrounded the fort. Still the Cree did not sound an alarm. They watched from the sidelines.

Attack on Moose Factory

Darkness fell. The Frenchmen surrounded the log fence around Moose Factory. This wall was 5.5 metres high. It was protected by a cannon at each corner. In the centre of the fort was a three-storey building. It was armed with four cannons. There were large main entrance doors at the front. Inside the fort, 16 men were sleeping in their quarters. Their leader was Governor John Bridgar. He had left the day before to sail to Rupert's House. Most of the officers had gone with him.

Two of the brothers, Pierre d'Iberville and Jacques de Sainte Helene, led the attack. While the HBC men slept, they tiptoed inside. They roped the cannons together. Then they slipped out again.

De Troyes got his men in position. Rough ladders were set up to scale the walls. They were ready for battle. De Troyes gave the word to attack. The stillness of night was shattered. The commandos shouted the war whoop of the Iroquois. They swarmed over the walls and through the front door. A chief gunner bravely fought from his post. D'Iberville killed him. The rest of the HBC men put up little resistance. They weren't soldiers. They were company workers. They surrendered. The battle took only half an hour.

The commando troops took back one of their old sailing ships, *La Sainte-Anne*. It had been seized by the HBC. The ship became a holding cell for the HBC prisoners. Forty Frenchmen were left to guard Moose Factory.

Attack on Rupert's House

The commandos moved on toward Rupert's House. It was 120 kilometres from Moose Factory, along the east coast of James Bay. De Sainte-Helene was in charge of the scouting mission. He returned on July 2. He said the way was clear for their second attack. Pierre d'Iberville led the troops. They headed out in birch-bark war canoes and sighted the fort. The HBC ship, the *Craven*, was lying at anchor nearby. They attacked at night. There wasn't much of a fight. The troops captured Rupert's House

Meanwhile, d'Iberville silently boarded the *Craven*. A HBC sailor was sleeping at anchor watch. D'Iberville killed him. Then he used an emergency signal known to all sailors. He stamped his feet to wake up the crew and get them to the deck. Crew members raced up the companionway. D'Iberville killed three Englishmen with the blunt end of his musket. The rest quickly surrendered.

All the prisoners were taken back to Moose Factory. Governor Bridgar was one of the prisoners. Bridgar was a prisoner of the French once again. It was the second time in four years. Rupert's House was looted. The furniture and valuables were loaded on the *Craven*. The fort was destroyed.

D'Iberville sailed the *Craven* to Moose Factory. He prepared it for an assault on Fort Albany.

Attack on Fort Albany

Back at Moose Factory, de Troyes and his commanders planned their raid on Fort Albany. It was the most protected of the Hudson Bay forts. It had 43 guns, log walls, and four cannon bastions. In mid-July, the French commandos headed out. They carried troops and equipment on the two captured ships. They were *La Sainte-Anne* and the *Craven*. Locating Fort Albany was not easy. It could not be seen from the water. It was on a sheltered inlet a short distance up the Albany River. This was a tricky problem for the French. They were ready to attack ... but could not find the fort.

They were ready to give up the search. Then the English fired their daily sunset salute. That gave away their location. De Troyes and d'Iberville set to work. They had heavy siege guns that had been captured from Rupert's House. These guns were mounted on the frozen gravel outside the fort's walls. Then 140 shots were fired.

Governor Sergeant of Fort Albany was sitting down to a glass of wine with supper when the attack started. Some say the governor had expected the French. Hours before, two Native people had warned him of the attack. They had told him that both Moose Factory and Rupert's House had fallen. He prepared Fort Albany to stand a siege. He told everyone to be brave.

The fort was bombarded for two days. From time to time, the English shot back with cannon fire. The first death occurred on the evening of the second day. A HBC servant was killed. The HBC men were scared. Sergeant overheard his chief gunner, Elias Turner, talking to his pals. He told them he wanted to surrender to the mercy of the French. Governor Sergeant feared mutiny. He drew his pistol and threatened to kill Turner if he left his post.

The French brought their cannon closer to the fort while it was dark. They fired a series of heavy balls that struck the **bastions**. At one point, the French shouted, "Vive le Roi, vive le Roi" ("Long live the King"). The English were frightened. They repeated the shout. They wanted to calm their attackers. The French thought they were being defiant. They increased the gunfire.

Both sides knew there would be no reinforcements. No extra food, supplies, or weapons would be coming. At last, the HBC chaplain came through the gate. He carried a white flag. He arranged for Governor Sergeant to meet with de Troyes.

Sergeant wanted to talk with de Troyes in the middle of the Albany River. Their two small boats set out. One came from each river bank. Sergeant wanted to show good manners. He had a bottle of good Spanish wine tucked under his arm. They met in the middle of the river. Sergeant suggested the two leaders drink a toast to their kings. They did.

De Troyes tried to show that he was powerful with a strong force behind him. He hoped the governor wouldn't notice how weakened his men were. It had been a long journey from Montreal. That trek and three raids had left his men hungry and tired. They could easily be overrun. Sergeant was too concerned about saving himself and his family. He did not notice their condition. The two leaders agreed on the terms of the English surrender.

Sergeant agreed to surrender the fort the next morning, July 26. He would keep his personal possessions, sidearms, swords, and his staff. Everyone would be shipped to Charlton Island. There, they would wait for the fall supply ship from England. De Troyes had to keep the prisoners from starving. He promised to provide supplies until the HBC ship arrived. De Troyes had wanted to find Radisson at the fort. He was disappointed that Radisson was not there.

Three Decades of Conflict Follow

It was an amazing military campaign through the wilderness. None of the French under de Troyes had ever been in that part of the country before. It was all strange new country. They did not know the layout of the land. Nor did they know the travel routes. It had taken them only 35 days to capture three HBC forts: Moose Factory, Rupert's House, and Fort Albany. The French held these three forts until 1693.

At each fort, de Troyes waved his sword. He proclaimed victory in the name of the King of France. Father

Silvie was the Jesuit priest travelling with de Troyes. He said prayers for the dead.

D'Iberville and 40 Frenchmen stayed the winter. De Troyes returned to Montreal as a hero.

Denonville was the governor of New France. He said, "The sieur de Troyes is the smartest and the most capable of our captains. He has the kind of spirit needed to command others. There can be no better example than the behaviour he demonstrated during our northern undertaking where he needed to be very clever ..."

D'Iberville returned to the bay the following summer. He went to bring out the captured furs. France appointed the d'Iberville commander-in-chief of Hudson Bay for the French. He was not even 30 years of age.

The successful commando raids of 1686 were the beginning of 27 years of fighting. During those years, the French and English tried to remove each other from the Hudson Bay. The northern forts were regularly captured, lost, and recaptured. It wasn't until 1713 that the HBC regained control of all of its northern forts.

Under the Treaty of Utrecht, the Hudson Bay and James Bay became the trading areas of the HBC only.

Chapter 6
Remarkable Adventurers of the HBC

Many men and women were a part of the history of the Hudson's Bay Company. This chapter will tell you about a few of these people. Their lives provide fascinating looks into the fur trade in northern Canada.

Prince Rupert

In 1642, King Charles I of England gave his nephew a special appointment. He made Prince Rupert his "general of hope." This made Prince Rupert commander of the military. The king was losing the **civil war**. He needed Rupert to turn things around.

Rupert was only 22 years old. His youth didn't matter. He was ready for the challenge. He was a warrior prince. He liked adventure. He led cavalry charges against the king's enemies and won every battle. His daring acts became legends. He liked to wear showy clothing when he rode his horse. One outfit was a scarlet velvet tunic, decorated with silver lace. He topped that with a feathered French beaver hat. He was a model of fashion. He tied a lace handkerchief around his neck. Other soldiers copied him. There was something almost magical about him.

His uncle was King Charles I. He adored Rupert. He made him his commander-in-chief. This gave Rupert more power. Rupert was a military genius. He developed tactics to strike the enemy suddenly. He put himself on the front line with his men. He once went undercover as a cabbage vendor. Then he drove a cart into the town of Warwick. He went to gather information about the enemy. He thought gathering this information was important.

There came a time when his tactics failed. Bristol came under siege. Rupert surrendered the city in only four days. He lamented, "I have no stomach for sieges." He was accused of being a coward. He was tried in military court for betrayal. He was cleared of any "lack of courage."

King Charles I lost the war. Rupert's military career seemed to be over. He left England and joined the French army for a short time. Then Rupert took to the high seas as a daring royal pirate. His flagship was called the *Reformation*. He raided other ships. He seized goods for the treasury of his royal cousin, Charles II. (Charles I had been beheaded in 1649. His son was Charles II. He had to leave England.) Prince Rupert roamed the Atlantic Ocean. His fleet travelled from the shores of Africa to the West Indies. His name struck terror on the waters.

One day, tragedy struck his fleet. A violent storm blew in. It wrecked havoc on every ship caught in the water. It was a seaman's nightmare. Rupert's entire fleet was lost to the sea. Over 360 crew members died on the *Reformation*. Somehow, Rupert and twelve others escaped death. They even saved some of the treasure.

After this, Rupert didn't return to his life as a pirate. Rupert became a hired soldier for the King of Hungary.

King Charles II was restored to power in 1660. So was Rupert. King Charles II gave him a lifetime annual pension of £1500. He was named admiral of the British Fleet. Rupert was a superb naval commander. He showed that skill when they fought the Dutch. He restored discipline to the Royal Navy.

Rupert lived a fast-paced life of adventure. In his forties, Rupert took a different direction in life. He became a scientist and an inventor. He also became a philosopher and an artist. He learned how to extract metal from ore and refine the metal. His books, art, his private laboratory, and his metal forge at Windsor Castle became his focus.

Rupert created the first torpedo. He worked on the first revolver and machine gun. His work led to the making of bulletproof glass. He helped create a new way of boring cannon to get a more exact aim. He made a naval quadrant. That made it possible to take observations at sea in rough weather. He also created a diving engine. It was used to get silver coins from a sunken Spanish treasure ship.

Rupert had migraines. To ease these headaches, he faced brain surgery in 1667. Rupert designed and created the surgical instruments for the operation.

Prince Rupert also got involved in the fur trade. He wanted to make money. He met with Radisson and des Grosieilliers in London. He listened carefully to their plan to trade furs using ships that sailed to the Hudson and James Bays. He liked their stories about the wilderness. He believed he could make huge profits with Radisson and des Grosieilliers. They needed risk takers to fund the first voyage to Hudson Bay. They needed Prince Rupert to buy into the project. And he did.

He was a man of action. He organized a group of his business contacts to put up the money for the first voyage. This group of men and one woman was willing to take risks. They also wanted to get very rich, very quickly.

Later, King Charles II signed a Royal Charter for the project. Rupert became the chief executive officer of the Hudson's Bay Company.

Rupert died quietly in 1683. He was 64 years of age. He was the head of a fur trading empire in a vast land. It was named Rupert's Land in his honour. It was a territory that covered over 40 percent of today's Canada.

Governor James Knight

Who was the man the HBC men called "Goldfinders?" He was Governor James Knight. He had gold fever. The older he got, the more he had to search for gold in the northern lands … until it killed him.

Knight worked with the HBC for 46 years. He started as a carpenter in 1676. He built and repaired the factories at Moose, Rupert, and Albany Rivers. He became chief agent at Albany Fort. Then he became deputy governor of the bay.

In 1687, Knight was charged with private trading. This was the most serious charge against an HBC employee. Knight left the HBC. Five years later, the HBC got him back. He was made governor and commander-in-chief. He had power over all forts and factories. He also had power over all territories in Hudson Bay.

At the time, the English and the French were fighting in Hudson Bay and James Bay. Forts were lost to one side. Then they were recaptured and lost again. In 1713, the Treaty of Utrecht was signed. It returned all the forts to the Hudson's Bay Company.

Knight was almost 75 years of age in 1714. He arrived at York Factory on September 4. His deputy, Henry

Kelsey, came with him. A few weeks later, an amazing woman came into his life. Her name was Thanadelthur. Knight called her "the slave woman." Why was she amazing? She brought peace to the Chipewyan. They were her people. She helped to expand the fur trade into new areas of the far north. Thanadelthur helped James Knight a lot. She advised him. She also gave him important information.

She told stories of yellow metal. These stories excited him. Day after day, he asked her about the northern lands. He asked about "virgin copper lumps ... so big that three or four men can't lift [them]." He asked about yellow metal used by Native peoples of the west seas. Knight even added silver and pearls to his search for mines. He talked about gold and minerals with Thanadelthur all the time. She told him about seeing and handling the yellow metal. It came from islands off the west coast. She made a promise to Knight. She would go with her brother to get the gold. However, she died before she could make the journey.

A year later, Knight went back in England. He had to talk to the HBC Committee. He needed money to pay for an expedition to find a northwest passage. He needed to find that passage. Then he could find the gold and other minerals to the northwest. He got the money he needed.

On June 4, 1719, Knight sailed with two ships. The *Albany* was under Captain George Berley. The *Discovery* was under Captain David Vaughn. They carried trading goods in their cargo. These goods included blankets, knives, mirrors, beads, and muskets. They carried brick and lime for building. They also carried supplies for about nine months. They brought lots of salt for preserving fresh meat. Knight expected to find a lot of fresh meat west of Hudson Bay. It is said they also carried "large iron-bound chests in which to bring back gold."

At 80 years old, Knight was the leader of the expedition. He didn't tell the captains any details about the expedition. The HBC Committee told them not to land at any HBC post. Nor were they to sail south into the Hudson Bay, unless it was to save their lives. The ship's crew headed directly north of 64 degrees.

No one in the HBC ever saw or heard from the crew again. What had happened to them? Two years later (1721), Kelsey found proof among the Inuit that the ships had been wrecked. He did not look further. In 1722, a report was made by Captain John Scroggs of the *Whalebone*. It said the expedition had been destroyed. All the men had been killed by the Inuit. The HBC wrote off the two ships as lost. They never sent out a search party.

Almost 50 years later, more evidence was found. It showed what happened to Knight's expedition. In 1767, the *Success* anchored at Marble Island. The *Success* was a HBC whaling sloop. The crew was searching for driftwood. They found a smith's **anvil**. They also found a cannon and shot. Another search found more signs.

They found the ruins of a brick building. A large coal heap and wood chips from the ship's timbers were also discovered. So was a human skull.

In 1768, Samuel Hearne led a search party to Marble Island. They found many graves. The hulks of two ships lay in five fathoms of water. (One fathom equals 6 feet or 1.83 metres.) There was a dwelling. Relics from Knight's ships were also found.

A year later, Hearne went back to learn more. He interviewed the old Inuit. They had visited the island when some of Knight's men were alive. Their stories told him of the crew's awful fate. Knight's ships were wrecked in the late fall of 1719. About 50 men had built a house. Many died during that first winter. By the end of the second winter, only 20 men survived. The following summer, five men were still alive. The Inuit told the sad story of the last two men on the island. The two men often went to the top of a rock. They looked for a rescue vessel to the south and east. Then one died. The other started digging a grave to bury his friend. He died as he tried to dig the grave.

During this time, trading vessels from York were sailing along that coast. They were about two days sailing time from the island. They didn't know that Knight's expedition was missing. No one had told them. No one seemed to care.

Mystery still surrounds the Knight expedition on Marble Island. Why did Knight go there? Was he too proud to seek shelter at an HBC post? Why did he try to brave the harsh winter on Marble Island without winter clothing? Did a storm drive the ships into the cove for safety? Then, did it seal them in with ice? What really happened?

Marble Island is a barren, rock island. There are no trees. It is 483 kilometres from Churchill River and 25 kilometres from the mainland. There are no animals for fresh meat. Winter there is harsh and windy.

An Inuit legend is told about Marble Island. An old woman on the iceberg had a final wish. She wanted to die on land. The spirits answered her plea. They transformed the iceberg into Marble Island. First-time visitors must not walk on the land. This is done out of respect for the Inuit legend. They must crawl ashore. This is to avoid offending the spirits of the dead who dwell there.

Henry Kelsey

Henry Kelsey was just 17 years old in 1687. He was sent on his first wilderness journey for the Hudson's Bay Company. He had to deliver letters from York Factory to Fort Severn. It was a 320-kilometre trek.

Kelsey did such a great job that the HBC had another place in mind for him. The next summer, they sent Kelsey and Thomas Savage to the edge of Barren Lands. This area was north of Churchill River. The shore still had ice. They were to bring trade to the northern Native peoples.

The two young men began to worry about the success of their mission. They had searched for 320 kilometres. They hadn't seen any Native peoples. At that time of year, the mosquitoes were starving. And there was no place to hide.

It was a long, tough journey. It took them six weeks. At the end, Kelsey had to shoot three waterfalls on a raft. He had to get over them. He had to reach his ship's pickup point on the Churchill River.

This trip was just a start. The next year, he went on a two-year mission. The HBC wanted to travel inland for trade. Kelsey was chosen to travel west. He would go deeper into native country than anyone else. His mission was not just to explore. He was to meet with native groups and invite them to trade with the HBC. He carried tobacco from Brazil. He also carried glass beads, hatchets, and kettles.

Kelsey was a good choice. He spoke the Cree language. He knew how the Native peoples travelled. He also knew the customs of the country. He travelled with a Cree companion. They headed southwest from York Factory. They went to the sheltered bend in the Saskatchewan River. It is just below what is today The Pas, Manitoba. They spent the winter with the northern Cree. Then they headed onto the great plains of western Canada. They may have gone as far as Touchwood Hills, Saskatchewan. Kelsey was the first European to see buffalo (bison). He saw huge herds of buffalo.

This journey was also hard and dangerous. Kelsey didn't know the land. He was travelling among tribes who were often at war with each other. He tried to help the Native peoples make peace with each other. He even tried to make trade treaties. He went buffalo hunting with the Native peoples. Much is known about his travels because he kept a day-to-day journal. He wrote all his entries in rhyme.

Kelsey was the first HBC man to make an inland voyage. A Cree woman was with him for much of it. Later explorers learned that an inland journey by non-Native people would fail if a native woman wasn't with them. Kelsey knew his success depended on having a native woman by his side. He returned to York Factory in 1692. A Cree "wife" came with him. He made sure she was allowed to enter York Factory. There is no record of what happened to her. Later, Henry returned to England and to his English wife, Elizabeth.

The HBC received Kelsey's reports from his expedition. Then they were forgotten. The HBC didn't use any of his findings. They didn't place his travels on a map. Today, Kelsey's journals from 1690 to 1692 tell of early North America. They are the first writings about the life and customs of Native peoples on the prairies. Later, Kelsey was the first to record the Inuit and other native languages. He spent long winter nights working on a native dictionary. It was published in 1710.

Kelsey was an important man in the HBC's early

years. York Factory was captured twice by the French. He was there both times. There was a great sea battle in Hudson Bay in 1697. Kelsey was there. He was also at the surrender of York Factory.

In 1719, Kelsey led another expedition. This one was to explore the northwest coast of Hudson Bay. Two Inuit boys went with him. He wanted to learn their language. From 1718 to 1722, he was governor of all the company's forts in the region. Kelsey worked for the HBC for 59 years. He died in 1730. His wife and children in England were left in poverty.

Mrs. Sergeant and Mrs. Maurice

It was April 1683. Henry Sergeant was put in charge of all the trading posts in Hudson Bay. He was made governor and chief commander. He sailed for the Hudson Bay with his wife, son, and daughter. Mrs. Sergeant had a companion and maid. Her name was Mrs. Maurice. She went with the family, too. So did Mr. Sergeant's chaplain, Reverend John French, and three male servants.

Mrs. Sergeant and Mrs. Maurice were the first English women to live by the bay. They spent their first winter at Moose Factory. In 1684, the family moved to the HBC post at Fort Albany. Little is known about these women. Their first names aren't even known. No journals or notes were found about the three years they spent on the Hudson Bay. But they did survive. That alone tells of their bravery.

The HBC supply ship arrived at the bay in 1685. There was a message for Mrs. Maurice. She had to return home to England. Her father was ill and needed her. She packed and said goodbye to Mrs. Sergeant. In December, she boarded the *Success* to head back to England. It was very late for any ship to get through the Hudson Straits. Luck wasn't on the ship's side. The *Success* was wrecked on the northwest coast of the bay. Mrs. Maurice survived the shipwreck. She spent the winter of 1685–1686 at Rupert's House. She had to wait for the next summer's supply ship.

On the night of July 15, 1686, Mrs. Sergeant was without Mrs. Maurice. Life at Fort Albany had been lonely and a bit boring. It had also been safe. All that was about to change. It was evening, just before eight o'clock. Mrs. Sergeant and her husband, Henry, were sitting down for supper with their children.

The manservant was pouring wine in the Sergeants' glasses. Suddenly — *Kaboom!* — a cannon shot fired through the house. It passed right under the servant's arm. Another cannon shot flew in front of Mrs. Sergeant's face. She fainted. The French commandos had arrived. Fort Albany was under attack.

The fort was under siege for two days. Henry Sergeant worried about the safety of his wife and children. Some tell of the message he gave to his men if the French were to get into the fort. Every man must take care of himself. He would take care of himself and his family. Years later, Sergeant made a confession. They were not prepared to hold out against an attack by European troops. They had no choice but to surrender.

Two days after the attack, Reverend French went out with a white flag to end the siege. He arranged for the meeting between Henry Sergeant and the French commander, de Troyes. They met in the middle of the river. Sergeant brought a bottle of wine. They drank toasts to their kings. During that meeting, Henry Sergeant surrendered. What did that mean for Mrs. Sergeant? She was shipped with the other English prisoners to Charlton Island. There, they waited for a ship that would take them to England. Who was on the prisoner ship? Mrs. Maurice! All that time, Mrs. Sergeant had thought her maid was back in England with her father.

Instead, Mrs. Maurice had survived the shipwreck of the *Success*. Then she had spent the winter at Fort Charles. The French had taken her prisoner earlier that June. She had been wounded in the attack on Fort Charles. She was transferred to Fort Albany by the French. There she rejoined Mrs. Sergeant.

After the commando raids, the French waited for the HBC supply ship. It brought supplies to the bay once a year. The French planned to seize its cargo. They would put their English prisoners on board. Then they would let the ship sail back to England.

The French kept their prisoners on Charlton Island. They had to provide supplies for their prisoners. It was

July. They thought their prisoners would be gone before winter. Both French and English waited for the supply ship to arrive. They waited and waited. But the supply ship had become stuck in the ice in July. It never made it to Charlton Island.

There were over 90 people on the island. Food and supplies were running low. The French commander, d'Iberville, wanted to get rid of his 52 prisoners before winter. There were still two HBC posts under English control. He decided to release the prisoners to these posts. They were York Fort on the Nelson River and the Severn River Fort.

The French had repaired a wrecked HBC ship. They forced Sergeant and 30 prisoners on board. These included Mrs. Sergeant, their children, and Mrs. Maurice. They set out on a dangerous voyage to York Fort. The other 21 prisoners were all men. They were left on Charlton Island. In time, they followed d'Iberville to Moose Factory. The French did not welcome them. Some of the men went to live with Native peoples for the winter. The others begged outside the fort to survive. The next year, they left by canoe for the St. Lawrence. They were the first Englishmen to travel overland from the Hudson Bay.

At York Fort, Mrs. Sergeant and Mrs. Maurice lived through a terrible winter. The fort was already over-crowded. The arrival of the Sergeants and the others made it even more crowded.

Henry Sergeant didn't know it, but the supply ship had carried an order for him. It was to hand over his command right away. The order had been lost in the shipwreck. Henry still thought he was the governor and chief commander. He used his power. He made sure his family was well treated at the fort. People were starving all around them. Henry made sure his family had enough to eat. During that winter at York Fort, 20 of the 30 survivors from the Fort Albany raid died.

Mrs. Sergeant and Mrs. Maurice lived through dangerous times. Shipwreck. Commando attacks. Battles. Death. Destruction. Imprisonment. Dangerous voyages. Hostile environments. Starvation. Then there was a 10-week voyage home across the Atlantic Ocean.

No other non-native woman would step foot on any HBC post for the next 119 years. That was by order of the company ... that is, until Isabel Gunn secretly arrived in 1806.

Isabel Gunn

Isabel Gunn was from Orkney. She put on male clothing and headed for the docks. She boarded the *Prince of Wales*. It was an HBC supply ship headed for Rupert's Land. Isabel was 26 years old. She went as a man because European women were not allowed at fur trading posts. She called herself John Fubbister. She had just signed a three-year contract to work for the Hudson's Bay Company. Isabel knew that she would have to pretend to be a man. She would have to work in a harsh land she had never seen. Why did she go? The man she loved was somewhere in Rupert's Land. He worked for the HBC. Isabel wanted to join him.

On July 29, 1806, Captain Henry Hanwell sailed out into the Atlantic Ocean. The voyage was hard. The waters of the Atlantic Ocean were stormy. The fog and ice floes of the Hudson Strait were dangerous. One out of every three HBC ships sailing the route were lost at sea.

The *Prince of Wales* arrived at Moose Factory in the third week in August. Then, the Orkney men were moved to northern posts on the Hudson Bay. On August 27, Isabel headed for Fort Albany.

There, she and two other Orkney men were sent to Henley House. They were John Scarth and James Brown. They had to take supplies and trading goods to Henley House. They travelled through rapids and fast-moving waters. They loaded and unloaded cargo. Then, they headed back to Albany. It was a tough 19-day journey.

The months went by. No one suspected that John Fubbister was really Isabel Gunn. John Scarth shared her log hut. Even he did not know that she was a woman. Often, Scarth would return from hunting and find her sitting by the fire, crying. Scarth noticed that Fubbister did very little work. "He" always seemed to be sad. Scarth thought the lad was homesick.

The months went by. Isabel worried that she would

be found out. What if she was shipped back to Orkney without finding her lost love? One night, John Scarth found out that she was a woman. He told her that he would tell the man in charge of the HBC posts. She begged him not to reveal her secret. Scarth agreed to keep the secret. They lived together in the log hut as before. It wasn't long before they became close. Isabel became pregnant some time in the spring.

Life at the HBC posts was very busy in the spring. On May 21, Isabel and Scarth went with a team of boats to Martens Falls. They took the inland cargo up the river to the falls. They returned on June 19. They had a cargo of furs and castoreum. Three days later, Isabel left again to take cargo to Marten Falls. This time she didn't come back. She was sent to Pembina. There she was to cook for Donald (Mad) MacKay.

It was a long route to Pembina. They paddled the Winnipeg River and up the Red River. Isabel realized she was carrying a child in Pembina. The HBC post was on one side of the Pembina River. Its rival had its post on the other side. Alexander Henry commanded that post for the North West Company. During the last week of December, Isabel and other HBC workers went to Alexander Henry's trading post. They went to take Christmas greetings.

The others returned to the HBC post on December 29, 1807. Isabel was still posing as a man. She asked Alexander Henry if she could stay at his house for a bit longer. She knew she was close to giving birth. The walk back across the river might be too dangerous.

Henry wrote about the surprise birth in his journal. When Isabel asked him if she could stay, he was surprised. He told Isabel to sit down and get warm. Henry returned to his own room. Then he got word that Isabel wanted to speak with him. He found her on the hearth in childbirth. She had a baby boy. He made sure she got safely home with her baby.

Isabel named her son James Scarth. She stayed at Pembina with her son until spring. On May 28, 1808, she left for Fort Albany. Everyone with the HBC talked about Isabel and Scarth. Only a few words were written in the company's journals. No one with the HBC had suspected that she was a woman until the birth of her son.

At Fort Albany, Isabel was made a washerwoman. She didn't like this job, and she didn't do it well. But she did not want to go back to Orkney. Isabel and her son stayed for another year at Fort Albany. Then on September 14, 1809, the HBC dismissed her from service. Six days later, she and her son James boarded the *Prince of Wales*. The HBC ship headed back to Orkney. John Scarth always said that James was his child, and Isabel was the mother. He visited Orkney in 1812. He returned to HBC service at York Factory. Then he retired to the Red River Colony in 1818. He married a widow, Nelly Saunderson, in 1822.

Isabel's story is one of strength and courage. She

was well suited to the fur trade, despite the fact that she was a woman.

Thanadelthur

It was the spring of 1713. The Cree attacked a group of Chipewyan. Most of the Chipewyan were killed. A woman named Thanadelthur and two others were captured. They became Cree prisoners.

In the fall of 1714, they escaped while camped on the north shore of the Nelson River. Thanadelthur and another woman started travelling to the Barren Lands. They wanted to find their people. The Chipewyan were nomadic people. Their homeland spread across northern Saskatchewan. It stretched up into the Northwest Territories. The Cree were their enemy. The Cree lived to their south and east.

About the same time, Governor James Knight arrived at York Factory. He was to begin his term as governor-in-chief of the bay. The paths of Thanadelthur and James Knight soon crossed. Knight's job was to take back all of the HBC fur trading posts from the French. The 1713 Treaty of Utrecht had given these posts back to the HBC.

Knight was settling in at York Factory. Thanadelthur and her friend were trying to stay alive in the wilderness. They were cold and hungry. They knew they would not make it home by winter. They turned back and headed for York Factory. Thanadelthur's friend died on the way. Five days later, Thanadelthur came across tracks. They were the tracks of a goose-hunting party of HBC men. She followed them to their tents at Ten Shilling Creek. Their camp was just upstream from York Factory. She stumbled into the camp. She was starving and exhausted.

On November 24, 1714, a hunter took Thanadelthur to York Factory. Earlier that month, another Chipewyan woman had also come to the fort to be safe. She said she had been a prisoner of the Cree. Knight had called her Slave Woman. He had talked to her several times about her people. The Slave were a tribe of the Chipewyan. He wrote about her in his journals. She had important information about setting up trade with her people, the Chipewyan. Knight wanted this trade. He believed it would bring huge profits.

Slave Woman died on November 22, 1714. Knight was sorry he wouldn't be able to get more information. Two days later, Thanadelthur arrived. Knight was thrilled. He had another Slave Woman at the post. Thanadelthur explained that her people would not come to the bay to trade with the HBC. Knight listened as she told him they were afraid to cross Cree territory. The Cree had guns. She told Knight she wanted to help him bring peace to her people.

It was the spring of 1715. Knight organized a peace mission to the Chipewyan. William Stuart led the mission. Thanadelthur was their guide. A group of

150 Home Cree also went with them. Home Cree lived around the fort. They provided the HBC with fresh game and fish.

The group left on June 27, 1715. They headed for the Barren Lands. Their mission was to find a way to make peace between the Cree and the Chipewyan. Knight gave Thanadelthur and Stuart instructions. Thanadelthur was to tell her people that the English would build a fort at the foot of the Churchill River in the fall. Stuart was to look for gold while he was on the mission. He was also to protect Thanadelthur.

Their mission was upsetting. Most of the Cree left the group because they were sick and starving. Only Stuart, Thanadelthur, the Cree captain, and about a dozen of his followers were left. They came upon a horrible discovery. They found the bodies of nine Chipewyan in the bloody snow. The Cree had killed them at the edge of the tree line. The Cree who were left with the group were afraid. They feared revenge by the Chipewyan. They wanted to turn back right away. Thanadelthur talked them into waiting for 10 days. She would travel — alone — to find her people. She would return with them to make peace.

Thanadelthur followed the tracks of the Chipewyan who had escaped. She found them in a few days. She had to convince them to return with her into Cree territory. This was not easy. They talked for hours, then days. Thanadelthur's voice became hoarse. She was determined. She had to convince the Chipewyan to make peace with the Cree. She wanted her people to trade with the English. She wanted them to be able to trade without fear.

Stuart and the Cree waited for Thanadelthur. Would she survive alone in the woods? They were losing hope that she would return. It was the tenth day. Thanadelthur came back to the camp. Two Chipewyan ambassadors stood by her side. No other Chipewyan could be seen. Stuart came out to meet them. Then she signalled to the rest of the group. It was safe to come closer. Over 150 Chipewyan came out from their hiding places in the forest.

The peace talks began. First, Thanadelthur and the Cree captain talked to the Chipewyan. They gave their word that the Cree party had not killed the Chipewyan. It was time to talk peace. Stuart knew that Native people were great speechmakers. He was amazed at how Thanadelthur could use words. Finally, Thanadelthur arranged a peace between the warring tribes.

The expedition arrived back at York Factory in May 1716. The Cree and a small group of Chipewyan were with them. During the winter, Thanadelthur married a Chipewyan. His name was Lothario. He learned to speak English.

Thanadelthur kept telling Knight stories of her country's rich minerals. She spoke of broad rivers, straits with great tides, and of a tribe of white-bearded giants. Perhaps they were the blond Inuit of Victoria Island.

Thanadelthur knew she was important to Knight and the HBC. He needed her interpreting and guiding skills. She enjoyed and used her influence on Knight. She planned her mission to the Barren Lands for the following summer. But fate had other plans for her.

On January 11, 1717, Thanadelthur became very ill. She was close to death. She called the HBC's clerk Robert Norton to her bedside. He would have been her partner on the next expedition. She told him not to be afraid of her people. Her brother and her people would love him. They would not let him want for anything.

Thanadelthur died on February 5, 1717. She was buried at York Factory. Her life had been short. She lived just 25 years. She left her mark as a diplomat for her people. She also helped open the northern fur trade. Knight admired her spirit, her courage, and her intelligence.

Chapter 7
The Rivalry Continues

I n its first 100 years, the Hudson's Bay Company was successful with only seven trading posts. They were all at the mouths of rivers flowing into the Hudson and James Bays. Once a year, Native peoples travelled long distances to the HBC posts. They came by birch-bark canoe and overland. They brought their harvest of furs for trade. The HBC men waited for them, ready to trade.

Henry Kelsey had explored inland from 1690 to 1692. In 1754, Anthony Henday led an expedition inland. Other than Kelsey and Henday, no one had worked to expand the fur trade into the interior.

The HBC had been rivals with the French. That ended when Britain defeated New France in 1763. A new trading rival was making its presence known. This rival was more dangerous. It would bring the HBC into a deadly war. It would almost destroy the HBC.

The HBC began to notice something. Its fur trade profits were starting to go down. Native trading groups would be heading to the HBC forts on the bay. Competing fur traders would stop them on the way. Business was falling. Fewer fur-laden canoes made it to the HBC posts. In 1773, York Factory had only 8,000 "made beaver." From 1756 to 1766, there had been a yearly average of 30,000. A made beaver was the standard of trade in the fur trade. It equalled one good-quality adult beaver pelt.

The HBC knew it had to set up inland trading posts in order to compete. In 1774, Samuel Hearne was sent to set up Cumberland House. It was HBC's first inland post. Hearne set off in the spring. He chose a site on the Saskatchewan River where several water routes met. It was called Pine Island Lake. This site is now Cumberland Lake in Saskatchewan. The site was in northwestern Manitoba. It was about 95 kilometres west of The Pas.

Hearne and his men cleared the ground. Then they built a log bunker. It had a *plank* roof. They used moss to fill the cracks and for insulation. It was the first inland post for the HBC. The men stored their supplies in a warehouse at the east end of their shelter. Hearne knew

The painting called *The Pioneers' Highway*

the winter would be difficult. His men were not used to the wilderness. They were stocked with trading goods and supplies. However, the HBC men almost starved the first winter. They had brought along very little extra food. A large group of rival traders set up in the area around the fort. There were 150 of them. Hearne dealt with them politely, but he was concerned.

The new HBC post was successful. At spring break-up, Hearne led a group of 32 canoes to York Factory. The canoes were loaded with 1647 made beaver. Trade in beaver pelts kept growing. In their third season, Cumberland House increased its trade to 6162 made beaver.

For the next 50 years, the HBC traders would criss-cross Rupert's Land. They set up trading posts from the Great Lakes to the Pacific. Between 1774 and 1821, the

HBC opened 242 new inland posts. For the first time in its history, the HBC encouraged people to settle on its land.

The Emergence of the North West Company

By the 1700s, the HBC was hiring Orkney men to work on the bay. These men came from the Orkney Islands in northern Scotland. By 1799, most of the HBC men were from Orkney. The Orkney men had skills the HBC needed. They could read and write. They knew how to fish and build boats. These men were an important part of the HBC. Few rose to higher ranks in the HBC.

Then Britain defeated New France. A new group appeared to compete in the fur trade against the HBC. They were young men from mainland Scotland. They joined with the former coureurs du bois. A few Irish and American fur traders also joined with them. Together, they took over the control of the Montreal fur trade. The HBC men called them peddlars.

In 1784, the "peddlars" from Montreal formed the North West Company. It was also known as the Nor'westers. Nine different fur trading groups became partners in the new company. They pushed deeper into the interior of Canada. They challenged the HBC for control of the fur trade. They went against the Royal Charter. They often built their forts right beside the HBC forts. These men quickly built a competing fur trading empire. It stretched right to the Pacific Ocean.

The rivalry between the Hudson's Bay Company

and the North West Company became more intense. Both sides tried to get rid of each other. Sometimes the conflict became violent.

In September 1809, a Nor'wester clerk, Aeneas Macdonnell, and his men seized HBC goods from a native trader at Eagle Lake. Eagle Lake was northeast of Lake of the Woods. The HBC men rushed to save their property. Macdonnell slashed John Mowat of the HBC. The wounded Mowat grabbed a pistol. Ile shot Macdonnell. The Nor'westers arrested Mowat and another HBC man, James Tate. They were sent to Rainy Lake. Mowat spent the winter in chains.

In May, the two wounded men were sent to Fort William. It was the Nor'westers' post on Lake Superior. Tate was forced to paddle. At Fort William, Mowat was kept in chains 14 hours a day. His body became infected with boils and cuts. But he was not allowed to have medicine.

In mid-August, Mowat was sent by canoe to Montreal for trial. He was bound in chains. The voyage took five weeks. He was found guilty and sentenced to six months in jail. He was also branded on his left thumb. By the time he was released, he was insane. He vanished in northern New York.

There was more violence. Rivals ambushed each other. Traders hunted traders. Traders were kidnapped. Forts were seized. Wives and children were terrorized. Finally, the two enemies were pushed to an all-out war.

Lord Selkirk tried to start the Red River settlement in Rupert's Land.

The Red River Colony

The Hudson's Bay Company controlled a huge area. They controlled the land, the people, and the resources. Native peoples lived on the land. There were no plans for European colonies or settlements. Then Lord Selkirk decided to buy a grant of land in Rupert's Land from the HBC. He planned to give the land to poor Scottish farmers. Selkirk wanted to help these farmers find land to farm. North America had land to spare.

How could Selkirk get land that was controlled by the HBC? He bought enough stock that he gained control of the HBC. Then he got a grant from the HBC for a huge piece of land in the Red River area. The land covered 300,000 square kilometres. It was along the banks of the Red River in what is now Manitoba, North Dakota, Minnesota, and Saskatchewan. As part of the grant, Selkirk also gained power to control the people living in the area. These included Europeans, Métis, and Native peoples.

The Métis

There was a problem. The granted land already was homeland to the Métis. They were the children of native mothers and Scottish or French fathers. Some of the men took their native wives and children with them when they left and settled elsewhere. Most did not.

The Métis lived in the Red River area. They provided the Nor'westers with pemmican. This was the food staple of the Native peoples. The North West Company bought the pemmican from the Métis. They used it for their **voyageurs** and trading posts. They needed this pemmican to survive. It provided lots of nourishment. It also weighed little and took up little space when stored.

Women prepared pemmican. They cut the buffalo meat into thin strips. Then they dried it in the sun. When it was dry, it was pounded into a powder on a buffalo hide. Then this powder was mixed with buffalo grease. Berries were used to add flavour. The women used cranberries, saskatoons, and blueberries. The final step was to sew the pemmican into 42-kilogram bags of buffalo hide. Forty-two kilograms was the weight that voyageurs carried per load over portages. Pemmican was perfect for the peddlars and voyageurs to carry. It could be eaten raw. It could be broiled over a campfire. It could be used to make stew or chowder.

The Métis and the North West Company did not want British settlement in the Red River region. The Nor'westers thought of the Red River area as their land. The settlement would run alongside their main water-routes to the Athabasca River. The North West Company suspected the HBC was in on the plan to drive them out of the area. The Métis feared the settlers would compete for the buffalo. This was their main source of food and money.

The Settlers Arrive

Back in London, three North West Company men also held shares in HBC. They were Alexander Mackay, Edward Ellice, and Simon McGillivray. They tried to stop Selkirk's plan for settlement. Ellice warned Selkirk that the Nor'westers might destroy the colony. Ellice thought they would commit any crime if people got in the way of their hold on the fur trade.

Selkirk did not listen. Selkirk's first group of settlers arrived at Hudson Bay in 1811. It was just before freeze-up. Their first winter was terrible. They had to go to York Factory first. Then they were sent on to Port Nelson. The settlers had no shelter or supplies. Many starved or froze. Scurvy killed others. There had been 105 settlers in the group when they arrived. In the spring, only 22 were left to travel down from Hudson Bay to the Red River area. There, they built a fort called Fort Douglas.

Another group arrived in October. When they arrived in the settlement area, no shelter was ready for them. The first group had only arrived a few months before. Everyone was starving. They couldn't help the new group of settlers. That winter, the settlers bought pemmican from the North West Company. The following summer, the settlers tried farming. Their crops failed. Another winter passed. There was little food. People feared they would starve.

Things got worse on January 8, 1814. Miles Macdonnell was the colony's governor. He proclaimed that no one could take pemmican out of the colony. Later, Sheriff John Spencer took 490 bags of pemmican from the North West Company.

The Nor'westers relied on pemmican when they travelled inland to trade furs. The North West Company worked out of Montreal. Each spring their canoes left with goods and provisions for Fort William or for other inland posts. Sometimes it would be a two or three month canoe trip to the north. The Nor'westers could not use the Hudson Bay for transport. They had to transport their furs to Fort William and then on to Montreal.

Fort William was the major point for North West Company shipments. Supplies and goods were shipped there. Then they were transported inland. Furs were transported from inland posts to Fort William. Then they were shipped to Montreal and on to England.

The North West Company needed pemmican. They could not let their supply routes be disrupted. Nor could they let their pemmican be taken. The Nor'westers struck back against the governor's pemmican ban. They decided to destroy the Red River Colony. They planned to remove its leaders. Then they would scatter the settlers. Duncan Cameron was a Nor'wester. He pretended to be a military officer. He ordered the settlers to leave the colony at once. He promised them a better life in Upper Canada. There were 200 settlers. A large group of 140 were to go with him to Fort William. The other 60 fled to Hudson Bay. Then Cameron burned the colony.

The colonists spent some time at Fort William. Then the Nor'westers loaded them into heavy open boats. They forced them to row across Lake Superior and down Lake Huron to reach Upper Canada.

The Red River Colony was set up again the next year in 1815. The Nor'westers were sure the HBC wanted to destroy them. Violence erupted at Seven Oaks. It was just outside of the HBC's Fort Douglas.

The Massacre at Seven Oaks

It was June 18, 1816. Jean-Baptiste Lagimodière was a freetrader. He had just delivered a message to Selkirk in Montreal. He was returning to the Red River Colony. The Nor'westers heard that he was on his way back to the colony. They sent Pierre Bonga and several Native people to stop him. They captured and beat Lagimodière. They took him as prisoner to Fort William. This was one day before the massacre at Seven Oaks. There, the Métis attacked and killed HBC Governor Robert Semple and 20 settlers ...

Cuthbert Grant was the Métis leader. The Métis set up their positions at the group of trees known as Seven Oaks. Governor Semple and his men came out of the fort. They headed toward the river bank. Grant sent Francois Boucher to intercept them. He ordered Semple and his group to lay down their arms. There were angry words. Then there was a scuffle. Semple tried to grab Boucher's gun. Grant fired. Governor Semple was wounded. That shot started a six-year war between the Hudson's Bay Company and the North West Company.

After the shot, there was confusion. More shots were fired. The Métis slid off their horses to the ground. They used their horses to level their guns at Semple and his men. Settlers were shot and died. Return shots were fired. The Métis stopped to reload their guns. Those on Semple's side thought the fighting was over. They thought they had won. They threw their hats in the air. Then gunfire surrounded them again.

Grant tried to save Semple from being killed. A Métis named Francois Dechamps placed a gun to the governor's chest. He shot him dead.

One survivor wrote, "In a few minutes, almost all our people were killed or wounded."

In minutes, Governor Semple and his 20 men died at Seven Oaks. The settlement of Fort Douglas surrended to Grant and the Métis.

After the attack, the North West Company gave gifts to the Métis. These gifts were a reward for their service during the attack. They also took six settlers as prisoners. They took them back to Fort William. Some were bound in chains during the long canoe trip.

Selkirk learned about the gifts given to the Métis. He was sure that the North West Company had a part in the murders. This launched a war of words. Both Selkirk and the North West Company published arguments about the reason the Métis gifts were given.

Seizure of Fort William

Selkirk heard about the massacre at Seven Oaks. As soon as he heard, he headed to Fort William. He led a unit of British soldiers. He also had with him 100 European armed soldiers. They were hired soldiers. They would get free land close to the Red River in exchange for their services. On August 12, Selkirk's fleet of canoes and boats entered the Kaministiquia River. Drums, pipes, and trumpets played as they paddled past the fort. The people of Fort William watched in silence ... and waited.

Selkirk got right to work. The Nor'westers had to release the Red River prisoners. He arrested William McGillivray for "conspiracy, treason, and being an accessory to murder." He was the North West Company's chief executive officer. McGillivray didn't want any bloodshed. He surrendered peacefully. Then 50 or 60 of Selkirk's soldiers stormed the fort. They captured the other North West Company partners there.

Lieutenant Friederich von Graffenried was the commander of the hired soldiers. He wrote about the attack. "Our men ... were in no mood to fool around, and broke down the gate. Fortunately no shot was fired. Otherwise we could not have held our men back from plundering. Likely, blood would have been spilled."

The soldiers guarded the fort's papers for the night. During the night, the partners gathered their papers by the armfuls. They burned them in every fireplace they could. When Selkirk learned what had happened, he was angry. He ordered a complete search of the fort. Hidden loaded guns and stashed gunpowder were found. He ordered the seizure of Fort William.

A few days later, Selkirk assigned the Iroquois to canoe crews. He told them to get the canoes ready. They would transport the Nor'westers' partners to Upper Canada for trial. He sent the prisoners out on Lake Superior on August 17. McGillivray warned Selkirk that one of the canoes was overloaded. It put lives at risk. Selkirk refused to listen. On August 26, gale force winds hit the canoes. The overloaded canoe tipped over in Lake Superior. Nine men drowned.

Selkirk stayed at Fort William until spring. Then he left for the Red River Colony. For the next six years, violence went on between the two fur trading rivals. Forts were destroyed. Both sides took prisoners. The fur trade business became an armed battle.

The courts of Upper Canada sorted out all the charges. When they were done, there were 29 charges filed against HBC and Selkirk. There were 150 charges against the Nor'westers. Only one charge went through to a sentence. Nor'wester Charles de Reinhard was sentenced to hang for murder.

The legal costs were high for both companies. The battles were ruining both companies.

Chapter 8
An Historic Merger

By the early nineteenth century, the North West Company was almost finished. The Hudson's Bay Company couldn't borrow any more money from the Bank of England. In 1820, the North West Company sent a group to London. They wanted to join with the Hudson's Bay Company. At the time, the HBC had 76 posts and the North West Company had 97.

The two companies reached an agreement. Two North West Company agents signed the merger with the HBC. The contract would last for 21 years. Then it would be renewed.

The HBC Wins Out
The Hudson's Bay Company had beaten its final rival. The merger gave it control of more land in North

America. Its territory became almost 7.8 million square kilometres. The HBC had control over most of British North America. The HBC ruled a trade empire from Labrador to the Pacific Ocean.

The Hudson's Bay Company had won. It gained complete control in the fur trade. Who could manage the huge new Hudson's Bay Company? George Simpson was a short, red-headed clerk from London, England. He joined the HBC in 1820. His first posting was Fort Wedderburn. It was the centre of the fur trading war. Five years later, in 1826, he became governor for all HBC's operations in Rupert's Land. For the next 40 years, he ruled the company. He earned the nickname, The Little Emperor.

Simpson had a simple goal. He wanted to make money for the HBC. First, he reorganized the company. He cut the number of workers by 60 percent. He closed trading posts. He wanted to cut costs and make the HBC run well. He had lots of energy, and he led a fast pace. He moved across the continent by express canoe, by horseback, by boat, and by snowshoes. Whatever it took to reach HBC posts, he did it.

Simpson ruled one of the largest empires on earth. He led the HBC until his death in 1860.

After the Merger

The HBC made big profits after the merger. It expanded its operations to link California, Russia, Hawaii, and

HBC's trading post at Fort Edmonton, 1886

China. The HBC could see that there would be fewer profits to be made from the fur trade. It looked for new ways to make money. There was maritime shipping and selling wood to the Royal Navy.

The HBC even thought about ice trading. James Douglas was the HBC's chief agent on the Pacific coast in 1853. He signed a six-year lease with some San Francisco businessmen. Their company, North West Ice Company, could cut glacial ice on all coasts controlled by HBC. They paid the HBC a yearly rent of $14,000. The North West Ice Company hired Native people to cut and load the ice. They had to be paid in goods purchased from the HBC. This was another way for the HBC to make money.

On their first voyage, they loaded up with 272 tonnes of compact blue ice from Frederick Sound (now Alaska). They hired 500 Tlingit from the Stikine River as workers. They had to cut a channel for the ship. Imagine cutting through 3.2 kilometres of solid ice! Then they carried the blocks of ice on their shoulders from the iceberg to the ship. The iceberg was about 1555 metres away from the ship. The labourers had no shoes or stockings to protect them from the cold.

The first shipment of ice sold quickly in San Francisco. Soon the group had five to seven ships hauling ice. They loaded glacial ice for new customers in Hong Kong and Hawaii. They built a large ice house in San Francisco. They talked about another one in Honolulu. Then, things started to go wrong. Too much cargo melted on ocean voyages. And there were problems in the company. It went out of business in 1856. After that, the HBC thought about entering the ice business. They had to drop the idea. Another company got control of the California ice trade.

Planning For Change
The Hudson's Bay Company was successful for over 300 years. What was the key to that success? It was willing to change. When the trade in fur started to go down in the mid-1800s, the HBC turned to selling other goods. They

sold coal and timber products to the Royal Navy and to other fleets. It operated its own side-wheeler. The S.S. *Beaver* sailed to its posts in the north Pacific. The ship became a travelling fur post. At many harbours, canoes of native traders surrounded the S.S. *Beaver.* They were eager to exchange their sea otter skins.

The HBC received its Royal Charter in 1670. Almost 200 years later, the company still ruled in the west. Business was good. There was peace in the fur trade.

The company knew big changes were coming to its empire. In 1857, British Parliament put an end to total control given to businesses by royal charters. The Red River Colonists were ruled by HBC governors. They wanted democracy. They wanted a government that represented them. And in 1858, the Crown Colony of British Columbia was established.

It was four years before the Confederation of Canada (1867). The HBC sent out word. It was ready to transfer Rupert's Land to Canada. In 1870, it let go of its rights of control. It also sold its land holdings to the government. The Hudson's Bay Company did not fade away. Today, it is still one of the world's oldest business empires. It is also one of the most successful.

Epilogue

The Hudson's Bay Company has had a long history. It has a symbol of its interesting past. That symbol is its white wool blanket. This blanket is known all over the world.

The HBC blankets became a regular trade item over 200 years ago. Monsieur Germain Maugenest was a French trader. He met with the London Committee in November 1779. He presented ideas to improve the company's inland trade. One way was to add "pointed blankets" as a regular trade item. The committee looked at some samples. Then they ordered 500 pairs of these blankets. They shipped them for spring trading at the HBC posts.

The "points" refers to how each blanket is graded by weight and size. Indigo blue lines were woven into each side of the blanket. These lines showed the points. A full point measured 14 centimetres. A 1/2 point measured half of that length. The points ranged from 1 to 6. They increased by halves. Each point represented one made beaver pelt.

At first, the blankets were hand-woven. Master craftsmen used handlooms to make them. Later, they were mass-produced on machines. The wools made a water-resistant blanket. They were strong, warm, and soft.

Over time, the blankets have been made in different sizes and colours. They have ranged from light blue to indigo. They have had green, scarlet, pastel, earth, and jewel tones. Native peoples used the blankets for coats and robes. They liked the three-point blanket. It had a wide coloured band across each end. It could be worn as a winter coat.

The white wool blanket with bright bands of indigo, green, red, and yellow was introduced during the early 1800s. It has survived over the years. This blanket and the beaver are symbols of Canada and the fur trade.

Glossary

ambassador: person acting for their government
anvil: steel block used to hammer and shape on
bastion: part of a fort made for firing at attackers
blunderbuss: short gun with wide muzzle
civil war: war between two groups in the same nation
cocked hat: hat with the brim turned up
colony: group of people who leave their own country to
    make their home in a new land
expedition: a journey for a special purpose
extinct: no longer in existence
mutiny: to organize a fight against authority
plank: made from flat timber
portage: carrying canoes on land to the next waterway
proclamation: official announcement
rival: person who wants the same as another
shareholder: a person who owns stock
sinew: strong cord that joins muscle to bone
voyageur: French Canadian canoeman or boatman

Photo Credits